Proverbs 19:21

"Many are the plans in a person's heart, but it is the LORD's purpose that prevails."

Copyright 2024 ©CharlesWeems
(PURPOSE UNLOCKED)

All rights reserved.

This book or any portion thereof may not be reproduced or used in any manner whatsoever without the express written permission of the publisher except for the use of brief quotations in a book review.

Scriptures marked NLT are taken from the HOLY BIBLE, NEW LIVING TRANSLATION (NLT): Scriptures taken from the HOLY BIBLE, NEW LIVING TRANSLATION, Copyright© 1996, 2004, 2007 by Tyndale House Foundation. Used by permission of Tyndale House Publishers, Inc., Carol Stream, Illinois 60188. All rights reserved. Used by permission.

Published in The United States of America

Book Development & Editing
LADY B. WRITES
www.LadyBWrites.Info

THIS BOOK BELONGS TO:

_____

PURPOSE UNLOCKED
"Identifying & Implementing The Gift"

TABLE OF CONTENTS

DEDICATION
8

BIOGRAPHY
11

INTRODUCTION
14

CHAPTER 1
Repurposing Purpose
(break-up)

18

CHAPTER 2
Unlocking Purpose
(breakthrough)

47

CHAPTER 3
Unleashing Purpose
(breakout)

77

"Life without **Purpose** is a life that's not lived!"
-Prophet Weems

DEDICATION

This book is dedicated to my hero, my father, Bishop Charles D. Weems Sr.

This book would not exist if he had not planted countless seeds of purpose inside of me directly and indirectly.

I am actively living and operating in my purpose because my father knew who he was and what he was created to do to add value to this world.

My father gave me an identity, a positive preview or reflection of who I was becoming &/or would become in my future, which is a man of purpose.

He was my first example of purpose, so this book is dedicated to him as a token of love for his leadership, prayers, and guidance.

Today, I am unapologetically walking in the realm of purpose that he desired for his life, and this is an absolute honor.

I am forever grateful to be a shadow of his heart's desire concerning purpose which has been passed on to me.

"A good father is one of the most unsung, unpraised, unnoticed, and yet one of the most valuable assets in our society."
-Billy Graham

BIOGRAPHY

Prophet Charles Derrick Weems Jr. is an Author, Speaker, Mentor, and the Senior Pastor of World Deliverance Church in Vero Beach, FL.

He is a third-generation preacher, an innovative kingdom leader, a visionary, and a prophetic voice to this generation.

He started his career as an enterprising musician, producer, and entrepreneur while serving and training under the tutelage of his late father and pastor: Bishop Charles D. Weems Sr.

After the transition of his father, Prophet Weems harnessed the mantle and captured the vision.

As an emerging leader, prophet, and author in this dispensation, his heart is simply to advance the Kingdom of God and promote Jesus.

He's a revolutionist with a progressive approach to ministry and the marketplace with a mandate to initiate change in all cultures and backgrounds worldwide.

"**Purpose** is the GPS of life."
-Prophet Weems

INTRODUCTION

Purpose is inevitable to those who are committed to discovering, pursuing, and embracing it.

However, the process of unlocking purpose can become overwhelming or exhausting, which has caused many people to feel depleted or inadequate.

While the pursuit of purpose should have initiated some people to run into it, they have actually run into failure, conflict within themselves, or complete humiliation.

This book is a key tool for those who are stuck or stagnant in the middle of life desiring to go deeper and to explore greater concerning their purpose.

It's a powerful source of spiritual guidance, inspiration, and motivation to those who need instructions, revelation, enlightenment, or biblical insight that will confirm or connect them to the key to unlocking their true purpose.

Purpose unlocked is transparent and relevant to both the spiritual and the secular.

It allows and allots every person the key to individual &/or personal manifestation.

Above all, this book is an additional lifeline to the unfiltered and uninfluenced mind of God.

"Life is not perfect, it's **Purpose!**"
-Prophet Weems

CHAPTER 1
REPURPOSING PURPOSE
(break-up)

Repurpose:
to give a new purpose or use to.

Seasons change, but for many of you reading this book right now, you have avoided the shift. Instead, you have decided to do what has become very common in ministry and the marketplace; you have a repurposed purpose. You have allowed yourself to remain complacent where you are, despite your time being up, your position being expired, or your assignment ending.

This happens for many different reasons, but one of the most significant reasons is because of the lack of understanding of one's purpose. When we are unaware of what's next, we tend to recreate, reinvent, or rebuild without a vision. We choose to occupy the space AGAIN, even if it does not birth any relevant or lasting results.

Proverbs 16:4 "The Lord has made everything for its own purpose..."

While this may be quite satisfying, it is also detrimental to your future, to individuals connected to what you have repurposed, and to the next dimension of purpose that awaits your arrival. Avoiding the shift usually diminishes your ability to move into the next or new season of your life, which is connected to your purpose. Repurposing purpose causes you to live in rewind but never allows you to see the value in maximizing your time and moving forward.

In some cases, you may even see results in an expired season of purpose, but you must be careful with what you perceive this to be. You may misinterpret what you see happening as growth, increase, or confirmation that you have unlocked purpose, and the truth is, you may be experiencing purpose denial. You must always evaluate why something is growing, what is truly drawing people to it, and where it is leading you next.

"The mystery of human existence lies not in just staying alive, but in finding something to live for."

—Fyodor Dostoyevsky

All growth isn't always God! Every crowd is not gathered because of genuine or positive reasons. Sometimes, people are stuck with you because they don't know their purpose yet or have missed their shift into their new season of purpose as well. It is vital that we comprehend when what was once a blessing has become a burden. Too often, we create soul ties with expired seasons, which causes us to remain unfulfilled. You can be tied to it and still, it will serve you no purpose.

Are you in love with a season of purpose that ended a long time ago? Are you still chasing behind the high of something that has already faded and withered away? Have you built an emotional attachment with a dead season?

Sometimes, you can become your own hindrance to unlocking purpose. It may have been sitting right in front of you, but you have been too focused on what was to identify where God is trying to use you next. Truth be told, the key component of unlocking your purpose is you.

You are the key that has the power to birth what you were created and called to do. Yes, God gave it to you, but it is your responsibility to discover it, pursue it, and ensure that it is activated. When you refuse to reposition your mindset, spirit, and humility, God will not give you the permission or release to manifest the next assignment or purpose for your life.

You cannot unlock what you have decided to replace! Repurposing purpose traps you in what you have built, what you have prayed for, or what you have a history with for too long. You must commit to breaking up with what was and permit God to release what's next.

Ephesians 2:10 "*For we are His workmanship, created in Christ Jesus for good works, which God prepared beforehand so that we would walk in them.*"

> "**Purpose** is the degree of accumulated assignments."
> **-Prophet Weems**

There are levels to purpose, so we are never stuck on one level our entire life. God has always desired to take us from one level to the next, from one idea to the next, and from one level of purpose into the next. Your purpose cannot be unlocked if you believe in recycling old seasons, moments, and ventures.

Can you discern what is next for you or have you been way too comfortable to sense your next season of purpose? Have you been extremely desperate to unlock your purpose but too consumed with where you are? Are you aware that you must break up with the old season of your purpose before you can effectively transition into the new season?

In order to unlock your purpose you must be able to identify if you are dwelling in a false reality. It is crucial for you to truly know if you have been repurposing purpose and giving it a new name. Unlocking your purpose will require you to stop holding on to what has already let you go.

God has not locked you out of your purpose, but your inability to let go of what was may have indeed locked you out. Before your mother's womb, you were already assigned a purpose DNA. God knew exactly who you were destined to be and what your purpose would be in the earth.

Even when you have no idea how purpose will truly manifest from one season to the next, God is already steps ahead of you. He has already gone before you to prepare the place, but you must maintain a consistent prayer, fasting, and word life to become sensitive and discerning of a shift when it is rooted in your life. He does not trap you out of purpose, yet you are locked out when you lack the ability to hear, obey, and submit to him.

"The **purpose** of life is to live it, to taste experience to the utmost, to reach out eagerly and without fear for newer and richer experience."

– Eleanor Roosevelt

When he speaks or reveals purpose, you must be very careful not to reject it because of fear, doubt, or complacency. These things will always eventually lead you to repurpose purpose, causing you to remain stuck in a place that has expired. When you commit to the shift, you make room for what's next for you and those connected to you or coming behind you.

Before becoming a Pastor, God was already steps ahead of me. I wasn't locked out, but I was definitely unaware of the major shift that was getting ready to happen in my life. However, the more I grew in God the more I became clearer things started to become for me.

I didn't have all of the pieces to puzzle right away, but eventually, as I continued to grow closer to God and be obedient to the steps he had ordered for me, I was able to unlock my new season of purpose. I was open and willing to submit to his will for my life, and I was not going to repurpose a season that was ending in my life. My transition into the five-fold ministry was painful, but it was necessary.

Unlocking purpose will require you to see, feel, and experience the unknown, and this is why many people abort their purpose. The thought of having to change anything, start over, or lose something or someone to unlock purpose can cripple your mind and decisions. I would've never imagined having to lose my father in order to shift into my new season of purpose, but God had a plan that needed to be fulfilled.

My father, who was also my pastor, battled diabetes, which was serious, but nothing that my family or myself considered to be fatal unto death. He also had a few issues with his kidney, but he wasn't sentenced to anything serious that threatened his life but he did take dialysis treatment, which he did well with. We knew for sure that he needed to maintain a healthy lifestyle, exercising, eating clean, proper rest.

He didn't experience any suffering from this that led to his death; however, he did have a stroke two years before he passed. After his stroke, he still continued to pastor, but he was not the same. His mobility was limited and he was not as swift or prepared to deliver or preach a sermon or to navigate through ministry moments and services as he used to.

I stepped up and began to do more in the church as needed or instructed, and the church engaged and responded positively. I preached about twice per month, and everyone could see the shift that was happening, even if they could not articulate it. I believe this challenged his confidence and affected him in more ways than we could comprehend at the time.

"The best way to lengthen out our days is to walk steadily and with a **purpose**."

– **Charles Dickens**

However, he continued to strive to preach and pastor the ministry. No matter what was happening with his health, he was committed to trying to perform his familiar duties as senior leader. It was evident to him that it was time to pass the baton, but he didn't and we were not rushing him to.

I never assumed that I was about to replace him, but God was indeed dealing with me and had shown me that I would be the next pastor. I was not as fluent to the degree that I desired to be, but I remained faithful to the post I was assigned to serve, and as I flowed, the response was a confirmation of what was to come. The ministry was beginning to shift and emerge right before our eyes.

There was a huge increase in appetite in the congregation for the prophetic. The call on my life as a prophet began to shift the trajectory of our ministry and there was a major change in our culture. There was a new thing happening for us all individually and corporately.

Guest prophets would come in and confirm the transition that was happening, and I do believe my father could see that his role was decreasing. Unfortunately, he was still trying to be who he was in a season that had expired. Although we may not have been aware of what was happening, we were all really committed to repurposing purpose.

As I began I continued to assist with the ministry and help navigate things for him and the ministry, my life began to shift as well. My business started to progress, I received a major financial increase, and seemingly, what he had desired and prayed for concerning himself was happening in my life. As God perfected and prepared, he could see that shift happening and so could I, but still, I never wanted to lose him.

"**Purpose** is that sense that we are part of something bigger than ourselves. That we are needed. That we have something better ahead to work for. Purpose is what creates true happiness."

– Mark Zuckerberg

Later, he was diagnosed with COVID-19, but he survived it, even when we really believed this could have initiated his transition. However, he had become very frail, and after suffering a stroke and Covid, his body was not as strong as it used to be. I watched him decline but could not accept that his time was about to be up and that my time was being birthed.

He was ready to go, but every time he would appear to be leaving us, my mother and I would pray, and God would keep him here a little longer; the spirit of death would release him! We didn't want him to leave us no matter how much we didn't want to see him sick or seemingly fading away. We loved him and losing him wasn't anything we could've ever prepared for.

I personally felt like his time on earth was drawing closer, but God was still sustaining him. Within a month, he had a health emergency that led to his transition. I was not there when this happened, but I believe I wasn't supposed to be.

I believe my father knew he had to go in order for the ministry to continue to shift and mature in its new culture. He did not want the ministry to be stuck or stagnant because his season had come to an end. Above all, my father wanted to see the ministry win as a whole.

Losing him was a painful hit to everyone, but in order for purpose to manifest, something or someone has to die. As hard as this is to accept, this is a truth that cannot be changed, manipulated, or altered. If the season or the person does not expire, there will be no inheritance, which is divine and valuable.

Transition will always birth inheritance, whether it be someone leaving or passing. A transition has to take place in order for purpose to truly be unlocked in my life.

The mantle had to be passed down in order for the ministry to go to the next dimension.

My father had to leave in order for the ministry and myself to fulfill its new purpose and destiny. His time was up, and whether we wanted to accept it or not, God had a plan and he had the final say. There would be no step up if someone or someone does not step down.

Although I wasn't necessarily the first choice to replace him due to my age, the questioning of my maturity and timing, my purpose was still being unlocked and God did not change his mind about who would be next. My mother took over for a while, but after having heart-to-heart conversations with her, and guest prophet coming to the ministry and confirming that I was next, later that year, my mother stepped down and I became the senior pastor. The shift was challenging, but it was a part of the process.

"Work with **purpose** is passion. Work without purpose is punishment."

– Jillian Michaels

When you are dedicated to unlocking purpose, there will be resistance. This does not mean run and hide or attempt to repurpose purpose, this means submitting to the process and staying before God until the warfare breaks. Never assume that warfare is a sign that you don't belong.

The challenge is not to change you; it is really to develop you. God always has a divine plan for the warfare you will face when the purpose is manifesting in your life. Never settle for repurposing the season you are in to avoid the obstacles you face to birth what's next.

From a child, I was preaching and knew that pastoring was my call. I pursued other things in my life such as sports, the music industry, etc., but not one of these things manifested or developed the way I would've wanted. God was preserving me for what he had anointed and chosen me to do.

The purpose over your life can't die if you are willing to navigate through seasons ending, moments expiring, and experiencing a failure that was ordained by God. If you really desire to unlock your purpose, you must evaluate what you are still holding on to. You must be willing to avoid repurposing purpose.

Now that you know what purpose really is, it is time to make decisions that will move you further into unlocking it. Learn to break up with what's familiar and become a student of your future. Commit to breaking up from old habits, thoughts, systems, and functions that are locking you out of your purpose.

1 Peter 2:21 "For you have been called for this purpose, since Christ also suffered for you, leaving you an example for you to follow in His steps"

Do You Believe That You Have Been Repurposing Purpose?

_____

What Have You Repurposed In Your Life?

_____
_____
_____
_____
_____
_____
_____
_____
_____
_____
_____

Please Explain Why You Believe You Have Not Been Able To Shift Into Your New Season Of Purpose:

_____

_____

_____

_____

_____

_____

_____

_____

_____

_____

_____

_____

_____

_____

How Has This Chapter Ministered To You?

"**Purpose** is not passion it's fulfillment."
-Prophet Weems

CHAPTER 2
UNLOCKING PURPOSE
(breakthrough)

Unlock:
To open or release.

I challenge you to open your spirit in this next chapter to receive impartation that can and will shift you into your purpose. There are many reasons why you may feel stuck, stagnant, or trapped in cycles that do not serve you, but I have been led by Holy Spirit to share a few things to help bring you clarity, confirmation, &/or deliverance. This is your season to reposition yourself to unlock your purpose, but first, you must be enlightened concerning the truth about purpose.

In order to really unlock purpose, you must really understand what purpose really is. Having a false reality of purpose can be detrimental to your ability to recognize or embrace it, so you must have a clear understanding of what it truly is. You will never be able to unlock what you can't identify.

The first thing I would like for you to understand is that purpose is a spiritual divine call on your life that has been orchestrated by God. It is his will for your life that he has ordained to manifest on the earth. It's not a moment, yet it is an experience that shapes and modes you one season after another.

Purpose was created to serve in the earth. It is an answer, solution, or obligation that God has plans to use us for. We have all been created to solve a problem, be an answer, or a solution to someone or something on the earth.

Your purpose is what God has assigned you to answer, serve, or solve. Your purpose is assigned to a need in the earth, and you are transportation for this manifestation to take place. There is a specific need that only you can answer, solve, or serve.

"There is no greater gift you can give or receive than to honor your calling. It's why you were born. And how you become most truly alive."

– Oprah Winfrey

No matter how much someone attempts to serve this need, it can never be delivered or done like you. It is not your personal agenda or what you desire to do in life, it is the divine order of God that you have a responsibility to align yourself with. Although it can be a reason or a resolve, it is still a prophetic assignment that God has designed just for you.

Although purpose is not about you, it will still involve you. You play a major role in purpose as you become the solution or answer to or for someone else. It is about the divine manufacturing of what you were created to release or birth on the earth.

Purpose is a mandate, an answer inside of you that has the power to unlock a remnant in the earth. Your purpose is utilized to unlock someone else's destiny. It is the very epitome of you; your spiritual assignment.

When your access to purpose is embraced, not only are you unlocked, but you unlock a community, a tribe of a specific group of people, or a nation. God created purpose to serve the needs of his people. Purpose births change, it cultivate, it delivers.

Your call, or purpose is about your contribution that you were chosen to execute in the earth. Submitting to this assignment births freedom to those who need the answer or solution that you birthed. Although many individuals believe they know exactly what their purpose is, they can't explain why they still don't feel at ease, satisfied, or fulfilled where they are or with what they are currently doing.

This has a lot to do with lack of understanding of what purpose is or the role it plays in their life. We tend to fall in love with hobbies or specific gifts and talents, believing this is our purpose without truly seeking God for clarity. Why should we seek God for clarity about our purpose?

I'm glad you asked! There is a spiritual process that must be embraced to really unlock your purpose. There is a popular cliche that says, "You must pursue your purpose," but this is not accurate. Purpose does not have to be chased, run-down, or pursued because it is actually looking for you.

Matthew 6:33 encourages believers to seek after the kingdom of God and everything else will be added. Everything is purpose! When you seek after him, you will run right into your purpose, which has been awaiting your arrival.

Purpose is not pursued, God is. When you chase after God, you will eventually come into a new reality, which is heaven's perspective, who you are, what you were called to do, why you were chosen to do it, etc. When there is no pursuit of God, there is no reality or revelation of you.

You will only live in your own desires, but never the real purpose that God has for your life. There is a huge difference between what you like to do and what you were created to do. You remain locked out of your purpose when you settle for what feels right and refuse to seek after what is righteous, which is the posture of committing to God's instructions.

Only God can reveal the full intentions of your existence, so when you are in the right standings with him, your access to embrace purpose will be unlocked, which is who you are and what you were created to do. It is in the pursuit of God that gives us divine access to what heaven has been waiting to reveal about our purpose and new identity.

"**Purpose** is the reason and the resolve of life; when and why."
-Prophet Weems

Seeking God initiates a clearer revelation of who you are as well as the value that you possess. The lack of this godly pursuit will only keep you trapped where you are, which is painful and uncomfortable. There is nothing more miserable than carrying what you refuse to gain access to, which is in God.

Go after God for what you need to unlock the next dimension of your purpose. Ask him questions and evaluate your current assignments to identify if God has placed you on the path to unlock what's next. As you submit and serve your assignment, purpose will begin to take its rightful place.

God is the key to unlocking your purpose, yet he has been replaced by many other things such as life coaches, success literature, and YouTube channels. While these are all necessary in some capacity, we should never forsake the posture of seeking after God expecting to find the right answers. When you go after him first, he will lead you to a spiritual midwife to assist with birthing your purpose.

It is not enough to hire a life coach, read purpose books, or receive a prophetic word without seeking God and becoming more like him. Someone can identify what you "maybe" called to do, but without God's confirmation, most times you continue to live full, dwelling on things to manifest while participating in the proper process of tapping into your purpose and birthing it.

We all have a divine purpose here on earth. Unfortunately, every graveyard worldwide are full of individuals who have never identified, understood, or embraced their purpose. Families take out the time all through the year to visit loved ones who passed on with potential.

Matthew 6:33 "But seek first His kingdom and His righteousness, and all these things will be added to you."

"You don't find **purpose**, it finds you, now turn on your location."
-Prophet Weems

This is an unfortunate truth, but it is a reality and could happen to any of us. The death of a person does not always reflect the completion of a person and sometimes, their transition is not because they had fulfilled their purpose, it is because their expiration date arrived before they could finally reposition for it. We should strive daily to pursue the kingdom of God and become everything that he has anointed us to be to ensure we don't transition from the earth full.

This does not have to be your reality at all, but premature death is the cause of death that many have experienced while living outside of their purpose. The truth is, this kind of death does not only happen naturally, but it also happens in the spirit. There are people, including believers who are living an aimless life with no intentions to birth purpose or they lack understanding of becoming anything outside of who they are right now.

They are walking around full because they have no access to what they are carrying and have no idea how to birth it effectively. This is one of the reasons why we are witnessing such a high rate of suicide, drug overdose, sexual perversion, murder, etc. What they were created to birth eventually became a burden that they are unwilling to live with every day.

Years before I became a pastor, entrepreneur, and relevant voice in my community, I lived a miserable life and could've easily died a premature death. I was not struggling or doing badly, but I was definitely agitated and irritable from day to day. I was full of purpose but had no clue how to release what I was anointed to release in the earth.

Living full creates an agony of pain that can't be lifted unless purpose is unlocked. Dying full may be the way out of birthing it, but you will never be able to live peacefully just walking around carrying it. It is better to birth it here on earth than to live with the agony of being pregnant with purpose until you die.

Many people transitioned in the natural that had never fulfilled their purpose, but my experience living in this torment taught me that it is more detrimental to live full than it is to die full. When you live full, you are waking up every day with assignments and visions that God is waiting to birth on the earth through you. This is why many people are so short-tempered, narcissistic, negative, and unapproachable.

Imagine knowing or living with the truth that you're actually better than where you are! The agitation and irritation of being self-denied of the potential of who you are by the fear or anxiety that challenges the reality of who you are. You must wholeheartedly commit to unlocking the champion and purpose in you and defeating the challenges that try to oppose it!

It is frustrating to walk around knowing you are supposed to really be a millionaire, pastor, entrepreneur, author, artist, etc. This is a heavy burden to carry around knowing it needs to be released, yet it is still locked inside of you. Just as a woman carrying a baby way past her due date, there is a great amount of anxiousness and fatigue that will begin to happen when these things that you are carrying are not birthed.

Before you are unleashed into your purpose, you will need to unlock it, so you may begin to experience something I refer to as purpose conviction, which is a deep desire or burning for what you are carrying to come out. It is when you have been operating in vain realms, entities, places, systems, or positions that you have outgrown. Purpose conviction will kick in when you have been functioning or working below your potential or the standard that God has created for your life.

Purpose conviction will tell you that you are greater than where you are and you will feel the need to be unleashed. It whispers to your soul that your life is on a greater scale than what you have been living on. You will begin to become frustrated about where you have been assigned or have settled to work or serve because there's more!

I too, have experienced this conviction while working a 9-5. I was extremely frustrated about getting up and clocking into a place where I knew my potential didn't belong. One day, I started to talk to my own spirit, saying, "I'm a star, this is so not for me!"

Jeremiah 1:7 "But the Lord said to me, "Do not say, 'I am a youth,' Because everywhere I send you, you shall go, And all that I command you, you shall speak."

"**Purpose** is like a waterfall; it never ceases to end until you leave it."
-Prophet Weems

Before my father's transition, I had a dream one night that I was attending a funeral, but I was sitting at a keyboard consistently giving my mother instructions on how to navigate the ministry. I was telling her how to do this or try that, and she responded, "Well, you come and do it!" I didn't know who had passed in the dream, but I had a blurred idea, but not any facts.

Typically, in real life, I was the musician, not the pastor, so my placement made sense in the dream, but not my instructions. My parents were the leaders, so navigating the ministry was their role, not mine. In the dream, I got up, and while I was heading to the pulpit, there was an overflow of people coming in at once.

This dream was a clear divine confirmation of my assignment to pastor. It revealed that someone had to pass in order for me to shift, and I knew this was God giving me another revelation of what was happening in the spirit and would later manifest in the natural. I didn't know when, but I knew for sure that God was speaking to me about my purpose.

𝓘 had no revelation or clear understanding of my purpose just yet, but I that believe this moment, this very irritation became a launching pad for me to begin my journey of birthing what was locked up on the inside of me. This dream led me into many sleepless nights and purpose was all I could talk about. I was literally expressing my heart about something that didn't exist, but I knew for sure that I was carrying it and I needed it to be unlocked.

𝓔ventually, as I remained submitted and faithful to my assignment in my church and my mother as a new senior leader, God began to confirm what I knew, what I dreamed, what I was carrying, and what I needed to do next to lift this conviction that I felt. The purpose conviction became so heavy that I couldn't carry it any longer, which is what led me to have the conversation with my mother mentioned in the previous chapter. I told her what God had revealed to me and that I was supposed to pastor our church.

It was when my mother submitted to the option of seeing the church grow and not die that I felt at ease. The weight of purpose began to lift as I repositioned into what God had already prepared for me. You can't unlock what you are not bold enough to confess and initiate to manifest.

Are you frustrated with where you are right now? Do you feel the agitation of where you have settled to serve, work, or operate? Do you feel out of place, unsettled, or in the wrong place from day to day?

Proverbs 29:18 "Where there is no vision, the people are unrestrained"

"Life without a **purpose** is like a body without a soul."

– Unknown

If you have answered yes to any of the questions above, this is indeed your confirmation that you are experiencing purpose conviction. God is not going to allow you to remain comfortable where you are. Instead, he is going to continue pulling on you to birth who you are.

Has God revealed your next but you have not revealed or mentioned it to your now? Have you been afraid to say what the Lord has revealed concerning your purpose because of the fear of being rejected or denied access? This is your season to unlock what is weighing you down, and this will require strength, strategy, and the ability to walk in it regardless of who doesn't comprehend or understand your purpose.

Your purpose is awaiting your arrival, but your transportation will be through prayer, fasting, studying his word, and applying wisdom and discernment to your life. God wants to reveal who he has sent you to serve. He is waiting for you to be obedient to his word, which in return puts you in his will for your life; purpose. You have a choice to find him or to find you, but it is only in him that you will fulfill your purpose.

Countless people are searching Google asking how they find their purpose, but the answer is very simple and doesn't take much more than a committed life and fellowship with God. Today, purpose has been extremely overrated regarding where we discover it and how we should operate in it, but the truth is this, no God, no purpose; know God, know purpose.

I encourage you to take him off of the shelf and make it a priority to draw closer to God. The foundation of purpose will always be at the feet of God. Refuse to live full and frustrated and make the decision to unlock your purpose through your intentional pursuit of God.

Do You Believe That You Have Unlocked Your Purpose?

_____

If No, Please Explain What You Are Needing To Help You Shift & Unlock Your Purpose?

_____
_____
_____
_____
_____
_____
_____
_____
_____
_____

Please Explain Why You Desire To Unlock Purpose:

How Has This Chapter Ministered To You?

"The capacity of **purpose** is assignment!"
-Prophet Weems

CHAPTER 3
UNLEASH YOUR PURPOSE
(breakout)

Unleash:
To set the purpose in you free.

Once you have a clear understanding of what purpose really is and have gained the momentum, ability, and access to tap into what you have been locked out of, your next season will be the reflection of you being unleashed. This is considered your breakout season; visions, dreams, prophecies, and promises are birthed or activated. In this particular moment of your life, you begin to look like what you heard, saw, &/or believed.

Seemingly this is the most exciting portion of experiencing purpose, countless people make it to this dimension and fail, quit, or become exhausted long before they execute their assignment in totality. Too often, we see people break out and rise in their purpose and fall shortly thereafter. Although this can happen for several different reasons, one of the most popular reasons is the desire for the manifestation of purpose and not the mission of purpose, which is what, who, when, and how.

Sometimes, we idolize purpose once it is finally revealed. The popularity, exposure, or gain from it in any capacity can initiate arrogance or self-righteousness, so we must be mindful of our character and integrity once we have been unleashed to walk in it. You must fully understand that purpose revealed is purpose ready to do work in the lives of others, not to build your stage to be praised and worshipped.

When we think of being unleashed or breaking out to operate in purpose, we think of fame, traveling, money, popularity, recognition, followers, and living our best life. Truth is, many of you who are reading this book right now truly believe that this is what purpose looks like. You are ready to take off into the possessions of purpose but not the process that it will require to manifest them.

> "The greatest tragedy is not death but life without purpose."
>
> — Rick Warren

While your purpose can and will lead you to exposure and increase, when you are unleashed you are repositioned to align yourself with the path that God will take you on to build your character, to give you the strategy to operate and build in purpose, and to ensure you are embracing the wisdom you need to make the right connections, decisions, and moves. If you skip this process, you end up repeating cycles, stagnated, and eventually failing! Being unleashed does not mean God is done speaking and leading you.

When God has unleashed you, it is not because he has equipped you for you, but it is because he has equipped you to help others. Purpose is the distribution of contributions, which means it is the very fiber of you being poured out on the individuals, community, or genre of people who you have been called to assist. When you are unleashed you are now allowed to participate in life's journey of supply and demand; your visions, dreams, and assignments are the supply that heaven demands in the earth.

*P*urpose is a mission! We can't desire to see the manifestations of purpose without fully understanding and submitting to the mission of purpose. When you are unleashed into purpose, God has permitted you to embrace your mission, which in return, will birth repeated manifestations in your life.

*A*lthough you may have unlocked purpose, you will never know how you will be unleashed. God is strategic and sometimes, just when you believe you have it all figured out, you don't. Even after all of the visions, dreams, prophecies, and confirmation, ultimately, God is still the only one who can truly unleash you to operate in your purpose.

Proverbs 16:9 "In the hearts humans plan their course, but the Lord establishes his steps."

"Maybe you've been assigned this mountain to show others it can be moved."

– Unknown

We are all unleashed or break out into purpose differently, so I encourage you to please respect your personal process and the process of others. God has a way of using your obedience to seek him to lead you right into purpose or he can cause you to have a Saul experience that will ensure that you fall right into it while you are heading another direction. Either way, whenever and however God wants to active and unleash you into your purpose; he will.

Although I had confirmation about the call over my life, I did not wake up and choose to become a pastor. Purpose was looking for me, but I was too busy trying to fulfill my own purpose that I desired for my life. I had no intentions at the time to pursue ministry full-time.

I could feel his pull, still, I was doing my own thing. Truth be told, I was lusting after my own agenda and totally caught up in it, in hopes of creating a great life from it. However, God has a way of having your purpose activation to knock right at your door.

I had a Saul experience! He was in a component of an assignment, but what he thought he was fulfilling was actually the complete opposite. However, the only way he was able to discover his true purpose was by experiencing the road of Damascus.

Just as I did, he thought he was operating in purpose or assignment until purpose showed up and found him. He had no idea what was getting ready to happen in his life, but after the fall, he was blinded and unleashed straight to his assignment. I too, had a road of Damascus experience.

The gym was a huge entity in my life that was fostered because I was not living or walking in my purpose, which is the industry of life. The entity fills the void of purpose, but it is not purpose itself. This was my void.

While leaving the entity, I had no idea that God was getting ready to launch me into the industry. I had a seizure that caused me to merge into multiple lanes. I wrecked my car, but I was still alive.

When I woke up, I didn't know I had survived a seizure, yet I thought I had just lost control of my car. I couldn't believe what had happened and my reaction was "Omg...I can't believe this actually happened to me." I had my own interpretation of my accident, and it was totally wrong.

Anytime we are coming into purpose, it entails us losing control of our own will, agenda, and our lives. The gym allowed me to be strong, lifting about 430 pounds without supplements, and I was navigating my life pretty well. I had strength but I lacked purpose.

They discovered I actually had a seizure and I also had a tumor in my brain growing for about eight years. I was shocked, but I believed God for a miracle. However, I did have to go through surgery.

I didn't have any insurance to cover me at the time, so I was sent home to wait for coverage. It took about three weeks, but during this time I was still praying for God to move his miraculous hand on my situation. I was anticipating God to heal me so I wouldn't need to have the surgery.

It was in this waiting season that I began to transition and draw closer to God. My prayer life, fasting, and faith all started to increase incredibly. God was unleashing me right before my eyes.

"When you find your why, you don't hit snooze no more! You find a way to make it happen!"

– Eric Thomas

After being called in to have the brain surgery done, I requested another scan to be sure they saw what they said, but they didn't. I had to trust God despite not having another look. I declared to the surgeon that I would come out better than I went in.

I knew by faith that this was not the end of me, but that this experience was connected to my purpose. My waiting season had birthed a new faith and I was assured that I was standing on a firm foundation. Even if I doubted the surgeon, I was never going to doubt God.

Immediately after surgery, I was up walking! They had never seen this happen, but I knew I was a miracle. God didn't let me die because there was more!

I was not pleased about how the surgery left me looking because I was big on my appearance, so this weighed on me. However, in the middle of the night, God begin to deal with me in the prophetic. I started to have a pattern of prophetic encounters in which I started to have dreams and visions, and God even allowed me to visit heaven.

I experienced many prophetic God encounters that transformed me in more ways than I can explain. I remember praying through the night and God started to purge and deliver me. He was repositioning me for what was next.

I suffered a lot of ridicule and indirect bullying because of how the surgery left me looking, and at one point, I didn't believe I belonged here; it was as if the earth was rejecting me. One day, I had a talk with God expressing my heart. I told him if I didn't belong he could take me because I was open to going to heaven after seeing how beautiful it was.

"**Purpose** is the reason you journey. Passion is the fire that lights the way."

– Unknown

In a prophetic vision, I was floating in the sky, and I remember God asking me if there was anything that I needed to stay for and I didn't. There was nothing that I saw that made me want to stay until I saw one of my sons weeping. That made me change my mind about transitioning into heaven, I saw my purpose weeping and it provoked me into embracing my reason for being here.

This was God's way of unleashing me into my purpose. It happened to me, but it also happened for me. What I went through was about being able to experience God during this sensitive and scary season.

Purpose found me, unleashed me, and I never went back to what I used to know or be. I have been determined to stay on the path that purpose provided for me spiritually and naturally. I have remained faithful to my assignment because of my assignments.

This refers to the people that I have been called, chosen, and anointed to serve. These are the individuals who need answers, solutions, or assistance from me. I have been unleashed, but I'm fully aware of who I have been unleashed for.

This is very important for you to comprehend and apply to your life. Unlocking your purpose is not enough, you must be aware of why you were unleashed and who you were unleashed for. Avoid getting caught up on the lights of purpose, attempting to be a star, and focus on being an answer to those who God is using you to birth into stars.

Jeremiah 29:11 "11 *For I know the plans I have for you*," declares the Lord, "plans to prosper you and not to harm you, plans to give you hope and a future."

Do You Believe That You Have Been Unleashed Into Your Purpose?

If No, Please Explain What You Are Needing To Help You Shift & Unleash Your Purpose?

Please Explain Why You Desire To Be Unleashed Into Purpose:

_____

_____

_____

_____

_____

_____

_____

_____

_____

_____

_____

_____

_____

_____

How Has This Chapter Ministered To You?

PURPOSE UNLOCKED
"Identifying & Implementing The Gift"

Made in the USA
Columbia, SC
24 September 2024